banana

guava

orange

mango

pineapple

avocado pear

tangerine

passion fruit

For Emma, Linda, Nadine and Yewande

The author would like to thank everyone who helped her research this book, especially Wanjiru and Nyambura from the Kenyan Tourist Office, and Achieng from the Kenyan High Commission.

The children featured in this book are from the Luo tribe of south-west Kenya.

Copyright © 1994 Eileen Browne
Dual Language Copyright © 1994 Mantra Publishing Ltd
This edition published 2003

First published 1994 by
Walker Books Ltd

Published by
Mantra Publishing Ltd
5 Alexandra Grove
London N12 8NU

ہینڈا کا انجانا تحفہ

HANDA'S SURPRISE

Eileen Browne

Urdu translation by Qamar Zamani

mantra

ہینڈا نے اپنی دوست اکیو کے لئے ٹوکری میں سات مزیدار پھل رکھے۔

Handa put seven delicious fruits in a basket for her friend, Akeyo.

اکیو کے گاؤں جاتے ہوئے ہینڈا راستے بھر سوچتی رہی کہ اکیو کو حیرت تو ضرور ہوگی۔

She will be surprised, thought Handa as she set off for Akeyo's village.

پتہ نہیں اُس کو سب سے اچھا پھل کون سا لگے گا؟

I wonder which fruit she'll like best?

کیا اُس کو زرد رنگ کا نرم کیلا پسند آئے گا۔۔۔

Will she like the soft yellow banana ...

یا خوشبودار امرود؟

or the sweet-smelling guava?

کیا وہ رس بھرا سنگترہ پسند کرے گی...۔

Will she like the round juicy orange ...

یا ملائی دار ہری آووکاڈو؟

the creamy green avocado ...

یا ذرا اکٹھّا اودے رنگ کا پیشن فروٹ؟

or the tangy purple passion-fruit?

Which fruit will Akeyo like best?

اَیو کو سب سے اچھا پھل کون سا لگے گا؟

"Hello, Akeyo," said Handa. "I've brought you a surprise."

" ہیلو اکیو" ہینڈا نے کہا"میں تمہارے لئے ایک انجانا تحفہ لائی ہوں۔"

"نارنگیاں! "اکیو بولی "میرا پسندیدہ پھل۔"

"نارنگیاں؟" ہینڈا نے کہا" یہ تو واقعی انجانا تحفہ ہے!"

"Tangerines!" said Akeyo. "My favourite fruit."
"TANGERINES?" said Handa. "That *is* a surprise!"

monkey

ostrich

elephant

zebra

giraffe

antelope

parrot

goat